Enough

Copyright © 2022 Kevin Dohmann.

All rights reserved. No part of this book may be reproduced or used in any manner without the prior written permission of the copyright owner, except for the use of brief quotations..

To request permission, contact the author at kevindohmannwrites@gmail.com.

Hardcover: 978-91-987710-0-8
Ebook: 978-91-987710-2-2
Audiobook: 978-91-987710-1-5
Paperback: 978-91-987710-3-9

Edited by: Kevin Dohmann
Cover art by Kevin Dohmann
Interior design by Kevin Dohmann

Printed and published by Lightning Source UK Ltd.

KevinDohmann.com

To my past, present, and future:
You are enough.

MAY

We are stars.
It might be a romantic way
to see us.
Us who fight mental illnesses.
But I've noticed this metaphor,
to see myself as a star,
helps me understand
how my illnesses
— because they are illnesses —
work.
I am surrounded by darkness,
an emptiness,
but still I glow.
People see me as warm
even though all around me is cold.
I burn,
my body in flames
and I'm complimented

over my bright smile
but they're incapable
of seeing
the pain behind it.
Few can see what's right in front of them.
A smile isn't always
a smile.
Love isn't always
love.

When you look up at the stars,
you see companionship
when in reality
it is solitude.
You still see the stars,
long past their deaths.
You still see them glow in the dark.
Just like us.

I am a star
because I knew
if someone would come too close,
they'd burn.
The demons in my head
convinced me

ENOUGH

I ruin lives.
My friends and family
would catch flames
if they got too close to me.
And they got too close to me.

I am a star, a burning ball of gas.
To die was the only way
I could stop the flames
to save everyone else.
No other life
had to be ruined
because of me.
Only me.

I am a star,
beautiful and bright,
with a darkness that swallows me.

I'm not sure when it started
or how it started.
I only know that it started
when I was around
five or six years old.
I don't know why
but I wanted so badly
to die.
So I tried.
And I tried
but no matter what
I survived
and I'm thankful
for it now.
But some days
I can't stand the fact
that I've been like this
most of my life.

I told myself:

When people have lived
too long in the dark
they start turning away

ENOUGH

from the lightest of hearts.
They close their eyes
so used to the pain,
the light in your eyes
can't shine it away.

No one can save me,
so I have to save myself
from this all consuming pain.

At 21, they say I'm too young
                when I've lived too long.

What I hate the most
about suicidal thoughts
and mental illnesses
is that they don't feel
like illnesses.
This is just how life is.
This is just who I am.
And I can't take it anymore.

ENOUGH

Don't remember the last time I showered or
enjoyed the silence that surrounds me or the
peace that was inside me.
Remember days without pain?
Eyes without rain?
Someday, maybe I'll remember again.
Silently suffocating because
I can't recognize who I am.
Optimistic lies like, "you're stronger than your demons".

No, I am not.

KEVIN DOHMANN

It's time I finish my story.
Say goodbye to the demons,
thank you for your company.
I must be on my way,
the ship is waiting
and I'm moving on
to the next chapter of my life.
For my story is not tragic
I am a human Icarus:
my wings brought me high
but just like Icarus
I'm free before I die.
So remember me in poems.
Remember me in photographs.
Remember me in smiles.
Remember me with the sun,
I am warm in her embrace.
I am not alone.
Remember me in life.
My life was never my own.

Until now.

ENOUGH

Eyes open to darkness
and I can see your boney hands.
Yes, I have met you before.
Since I was six, you've been
knocking on my door.
Sometimes you turn around
and sometimes you stay.
I know I will follow you out.
But Death: not today.

I'm shaking
in a waiting room.
Minutes tick by like hours
plucked from my skin.
Doctors
and nurses
walk around
avoiding
eye contact.
I think back to
Alice
and the Queen
thinking of six impossible things
before breakfast.
I haven't had breakfast yet
and I've thought of
a hundred different ways
to kill myself
on the way here.
This waiting room
should have an Alice sign
because we're all mad here.

ENOUGH

"Who is your emergency contact?"

"Who do you want us to call?"

"Do you want us to call your parents?"

No.

KEVIN DOHMANN

Why don't I want
my parents to know
I'm hospitalized
for suicide prevention?

Because it's my brain
not my body.
My brain is sick
and I have no energy.
My body is just anxiety.
My hands itch to hurt me.

If you call
and tell me you're worried,
that you're sad for me,
it won't help me heal.

If my body was broken
it'd be easier to deal with
"get better soon"
"hope your body mends"
"I'm so worried about you".
But my brain is affected
by your words,

ENOUGH

by your calls,
my body isn't.

Your words don't affect
how fast a broken bone heals
but they affect
how fast my brain gets better.
So I don't want you to know
because I want to get better.

I am insufficient.
I am constantly feeling
the necessity to become
the perfect daughter.
Who doesn't complain.
Who doesn't cry.
The daughter who is strong.
I punish myself because
I am insufficient.
I punish myself because
I complain.
I punish myself because
I cry.

    It doesn't mean I'm weak.

ENOUGH

A nurse comes to me
with small plastic cups.
One with pills,
one with water.
That's my morning routine.

KEVIN DOHMANN

When we talk about depression
we don't talk about
the depressing facts.
Like how showering
and brushing teeth
cost too much energy.
Like how we're tired
all the time, no matter the rest.
Like how we like to hurt,
especially if it's ourselves.
Like how nothing is important.
Everything around us
can disappear
and nothing would change.
We'd still be here,
sick.

When we talk about depression
we don't talk about
how hard it is
to talk about
the things that bother us.
How hard it is to open up.
How scary it is.

ENOUGH

Because maybe
I'm just faking it.
That's what my head says.
I'm not worth the attention
so don't give it.

When we talk about depression
it's an attractive girl
or a brooding guy
who look a little sad
which love can cure.
Depression isn't pretty.

When we talk about depression —

I don't know what people say
when they talk about depression
'cause in my family
it's an elephant in the room
stomping on my chest
and everyone knows it
but no one does anything to change it.

When I talk about depression
they tell me to stop.

That they don't want to know.
So I suffer in silence
while they're asking
why I'm so quiet.
Why I don't tell them things.
We need to talk about depression.

ENOUGH

Another day without visitors.
I should be used to this
but every time
the door opens
I expect it's my friends.
It never is.
And I get scared it's my parents.
I'm happy it never is.
But then again
they don't even know
I'm here.

A fellow patient
talks about us
as if we're well.
Healthy.
She waves over
a nurse when I disagree.
"Are we sick or well?"
the patient asks.
"I see you as well,"
the nurse replies.
"If I'm well," I begin,
"Why am I on meds
and why am I
in a mental ward?"
The nurse only says
"interesting" before walking away.

I am unwell.
Sick.
I'm playing chess
with my mind,
always one step behind,
playing for both sides.

ENOUGH

I am unwell
because I wouldn't
be alive today,
if I weren't on meds.
I am unwell.
I don't want to see my demons
as parts of myself.
I used to,
and I got into a dark place.
A cage.
The only way to escape it
is to separate me
and the demons in my head,
telling me
everyone will be better off
when I'm dead.
So I remind myself:
I wouldn't be better off
if I was dead.
I need me alive
in case I want to live
tomorrow,
in a year
or ten.

If I give up,
I'm losing my best friend.

I am unwell,
because that's the only way to get better.
How can I become healthy
if I think I already am?

ENOUGH

A nurse talks to me
over a game of cards
with other patients.
They talk about
support systems.
When it's time for me
to participate
I say "I don't have any."
And nurses being as they are
pry me open.
Their questions
scalpels against my chest
trying to reveal the inner pain
until it streams out my mouth.
"They've never been there for me,"
I say "they wouldn't understand
if they knew I'm here."
"You must have hidden it well,"
a nurse says.
No, I think,
the signs were all there,
and they chose not to see them.

My parents got calls from school
saying I was crying a lot.
I cried every day
for the smallest thing.
I came to school
with cuts on my arms
as if I fell
into a rose bush.
My parents replied:
"that's how she is."

ENOUGH

Every five minutes
a nurse enters my room.
I pretend to sleep
because if they see me,
if they know I'm awake,
I might need to talk
about the war in my head.
I prefer the war
over talking.

There's a girl at the ward
laying a puzzle by herself.
So for breakfast one day
I sit opposite her.
"How's it going?" I ask
and suddenly the two of us
finish the puzzle
and start a new.
And a new.
And we talk.
We complain about the ward,
mental illnesses,
suicidal thoughts.

We talk about family
and I tell her that my parents
don't know I'm here.
"I don't have a great relationship with them," I say.
And because I see her phone light up
with a call from her mom,
I add: "I'm happy others do."
She stares onto the table between us
and I'm scared I made her uncomfortable.
That she's just another person
uncomfortable with the likes of me.

She turns off her phone,
looks up at me,
and says "it's the same for me."
She says she doesn't have a great relationship
with her parents,
and she tells me why.
She tells me stories of her life
and her childhood.
Of her absent father
and overbearing mother.
I tell her about mine
and we cry over the Weasleys
because there's no Mrs. Weasley

ENOUGH

to take us in like Harry.
We finish three puzzles
before binging a show.
We share a love
for books and writing
and *The Good Place*.
I've never felt so understood
as I did with her.

        But nothing ever lasts forever.

Granny told my parents,
so they want to visit.
I tell them "no".
I tell them I don't want them to
so they drive up
to my city,
sleep in a hotel,
texting me.
They want to visit.
I tell them I don't want them to
they say "we want to be closer to you".
Again it's their needs above mine.
Guess even if I'm suicidal
they won't do what I ask.
Even if I'm hospitalized
it's their needs that win
over mine.

ENOUGH

The new doctor
has an accent
and a nickname
'cause the nurses
can't pronounce
his full name.
Only the first syllable.
Other patients frown and freeze
when he introduces himself.
I grin at him
relieved.
I've had this discussion
with granny
more times than I can count.
How if I had the choice
between someone
who speaks perfect Swedish
and someone who doesn't
I'd choose the latter.
If you speak in broken Swedish,
the pronunciation foreign on your tongue,
I will trust you more
in a superior position
because if you got to where you are

when Swedish isn't your first language
that must mean you're brilliant.

    Like my Opa was.

ENOUGH

Granny gives me a lecture.
My parents went to her
and said they came to the ward
and I didn't let them in.
I say "I told them not to come".
She says "they didn't tell me this".

Of course they didn't.
Because it doesn't matter if
I'm hospitalized for suicide prevention.
A nurse stuck a needle in me
on my arms and my hands
eight times to get blood.
My veins were too small.
For days I didn't drink.
For days I didn't eat.
Now I have supervision every five minutes.
I'm on three different medications now.
I'm tired all the time.
I want to die.
      I want to die.
           I want to die.

But my parents are the victims.
      Of course they are.

KEVIN DOHMANN

After breakfast on Saturday
my phone rings and rings.
I ignore it
until it's the tenth time in a minute.
I reach for my phone
and stare at the screen.
Missed calls from my sister Linn
and grandma and grandpa.
Did Granny tell?
No.
No.
No no no no no.
My parents know
so of course they took it upon themselves
to tell everyone else.

ENOUGH

I turn my phone off.
Go to the nurse's office
and ask for anxiety meds.
"You're shaking," she says.
"Do you want to talk?"
I shake my head,
and down the liquid.
I hate it. It feels like
thick mint mouthwash
burns my throat.
"Let's get you to the massage chair,"
she says and leads the way.
One door separates it
from the office.
"Just knock on it
if you need anything."
I nod, taking a seat.
It doesn't help,
because it doesn't change
the fact my phone will later reveal
more missed calls and messages.

KEVIN DOHMANN

When the medicine
has its effect
I call my sister.
"I heard," she says,
"why didn't you say anything?"
When I don't answer
she continues, "mom and dad are worried.
Saga, everyone's worried.
What are you hospitalized for?"
"Suicide prevention," I say.
"That must be hard,
I know mom and dad were up there
why didn't you let them visit?
I know they want to,
it's all they talk about."
This is the reason.
All these questions
pry me open
draining the little energy
I possess.
I'm here to get better
not to get interrogated.

JUNE

After ten days
the doctor signs me out.
Dad is mad
that I'm mad
they told our family
I was hospitalized.

He says,
"I hope you understand
that if you're hospitalized again
we'll tell them again."

So I say,
"I hope you understand
that if I'm hospitalized again
I won't tell you."

ENOUGH

I tell everyone to give me space.
To give me time
to heal.
To cope.

So I could focus
on getting better.
Eating.
Taking my medications.
Cleaning my apartment.
Get on track with Uni.
Spend time with my cats.

So I could focus on me
and my health.

I should've known.

June sixth

Also called: six days after I was discharged.
Also called: the day after my friends told me I look healthier, that I'm glowing.
Also called: the day I went to Uni to study for tomorrow's exam.
Also called: the day mom broke off contact with me.
Also called: the day granny told me I'm the one to blame.

It's funny,
so patriotic of you, mom,
to celebrate the day
our country became independent
by becoming independent
from me.

ENOUGH

I'm at the university
studying for tomorrow's exam.
A cup of coffee to my right.

I ate breakfast today!
BREAKFAST!
I have a timer on my phone
to keep track of my meals
so I don't forget to eat again,
so I don't forget to drink.
So I get better
because I want to get better.

I've been here, in this group room
for hours
and hours
and hours
and mom calls.
     I stare at my phone.

I   b r e a t h e i n.

I b r e a t h e out.

And I answer.

Mom says, "I'm mistreated."
Mom says she's mistreated because I haven't called.
I say "I told you I'd call when I'm better.
When I could cope better.
When I'm stable."
"I don't understand" she says.
"It takes too much energy," I explain.
She scoffs. "How do you want to do this summer
with the cottage
since we take your energy?"
I sigh
because of course
she misunderstands me.
But I'm exhausted
so I answer honestly:
"I'm going to focus on getting better,
so I don't have to get to a place
where I'm choosing between life and death
again."
"Have a good life then," she says and hangs up.
And I cry.

I cry because I'm shocked.
I cry because apparently I don't deserve better.

ENOUGH

I don't deserve "hope you're getting better"
or "hope you're feeling better."
Maybe those are myths
meant to heighten expectations
like Disney does.
Maybe that mom doesn't exist
for anyone.

Maybe I do deserve this.

KEVIN DOHMANN

To the silence,
to the sweet beautiful silence,
I have to leave you.
You've become
toxic
for me.

No, sweet silence,
don't hug me.
I don't want you
around me
anymore.

Please, please, please
   l   e   a   v   e.
You're a black hole
sucking me in.

To the silence,
to the sweet broken silence,
because you're not silence.

ENOUGH

You told me
you're actually
anxiety.
I hear mom yelling at me.

Yes, sweet silence:
she broke you too.

I guess this
is why it's called
"the calm before the storm."
I was calm
before she called.
Would I break less
if I felt worse?
If I awoke
suicidal,
would I be more whole?
I guess I'll never know.

ENOUGH

You're funny, you're kind.
You've cheered me on all my life.
When I felt down, you helped me up.
You have always been there for me.
I don't know how I can ever repay you.
I never doubted you love me.
I never doubted your trust.
But the world doesn't agree
that you're the best mom to me.
Even though everything said about a mom
reminds me of you, Granny.

At least it used to.

Hi granny,
mom just broke off contact with me
and you tell me
it should be expected.
That I should've known.

Thank you.
Thank you for your kind words,
for your compassion.
Mom abandoned me
and it's my fault.

Thank you, granny.
Now I know
which side you're on.

ENOUGH

In September 2015
I got ready for Uni
and dad called me.
"We're getting a divorce," he said.
"Okay," I said, shrugging into
my leather jacket.
"I'm sleeping
in the guest room," he continued.
"We drive separately
to work."
"Okay," I said. "How do you feel?"
He's quiet for a moment
long enough for me
to think the line had died.
"I think it's for the better,"
he said, "I think it's what we need
to be happy."
"Then I support it," I said,
"I just want you happy."
He was quiet again
but this time I heard him breathe.

"That's very rational of you."
I chuckle before silence engulfs us again.
"I assume Linn's not taking it well."
"She won't talk to me," he said,
"████ won't talk to me either."
"I'll talk to them," I said.
Dad sighed and I heard his smile
when he said "Thank you."

So I called mom
and talked to her
on the way to class.
She cried,
I barely heard her words.
I talked her through it all
but mostly I listened.

Tell me how much
you hate my dad
and how he broke our family.
It's okay, mom
lay all your problems
on me.
I am strong.

ENOUGH

    I can take it.
    But I shouldn't
    have to.

          I did that every day.
          I called her every day
          to make sure she's okay
          and I called Linn every day
          to make sure she's okay
          and I called dad every day
          to make sure he's okay
          and he cries, telling me
          he's happy someone's on his side.

          Was I crazy to think,
          when the time came,
          he'd be on mine?

I'm an idiot
because I expect
dad to call.
That he'd say
"I heard mom's perspective
and now I want yours."

Not one week
since hospitalization
for suicide prevention
and no one calls
and asks me
"How are you?"

Granny calls.
She wants me to fix this
so I do what I always do:
I put the family first.

I call dad.
He doesn't answer.
I call mom.
She answers.
I say, "I want to talk
about our last call."
"It wasn't a nice call for me," she says.
"How do you want to do with the cottage?" I ask.
"It wouldn't be vacation," she says,
"if you're there with us."

ENOUGH

Dad calls me back
late in the evening.
He and mom
are on the other end.
They're yelling
and I'm crying
but they're not quiet
long enough
to notice.
Dad says "I can't believe
you called your mother worthless."
"I never said that."
Mom says, "I don't know
if I can ever be happy again.
I don't sleep anymore
after how you treated me.
Cruel and selfish."
And then come the words
that tipped the scale.
The step over the point of no return.

"Don't count
on seeing or hearing
from us again."
And the line dies.
And I fall to the floor.

Apparently I'm crying
because my cats
are licking my hands
staring up at me
with their big eyes.
It's a reminder
I'm not alone.
I am loved.
I matter.
For two girls
I'm everything.
Maybe that can be enough?

                    I guess it has to now.

ENOUGH

I hate that they left
and the world keeps turning

                    for everyone else.

It's okay mom,
you saw an out
and you took it.
I get it:
I'd leave me too.

So it's time I do.

ENOUGH

For three years I've been
free from self-harm.
Now I'm aching to break.
I'm longing to bleed.
so I tell myself
that I'm not weak.
I can fight the itch
'cause I'm not weak.
I can, I can.
I'm not —

                                                     I couldn't.

KEVIN DOHMANN

I stand in my bathroom,
razors in hand.
Staring at them in the mirror.
Dad's upturned eyes
gray as my mother's.
I thank the world
there are no freckles on my skin,
the only one in the family.
I hate the world for my hair
for the thick brown curls
identical to the woman who left.

I scratch my skin,
pull out my hair
as tears fall
like raindrops
on my skin
dissolving the mask
of who I used to be.

Maybe I made a mistake

ENOUGH

going to the hospital for help?
Maybe I was just thinking of myself?
Maybe I'm selfish as mom said?

If I had gone through with it,
if I had taken my life,
I'd have died in a world
where parents don't leave.
So I take the razors
to my skin
sawing off my hair
as if pieces of me
and this vacuum in my chest
could fall off with them.
Is this how trees feel
when autumn comes?
The cold and grim,
making their leaves fall off.
As mine do.
As I do.
If I'd be a tree,
I'd be a birch
beautiful and scarred.
Alone.

The tree equivalent of stars
always bright
against the dark.

I watch my leaves fall thick
against the tiled floor
around my legs.

All of this has to go.

I'm not who I was yesterday,
I'll never be her again,
don't you understand?
I'm hollow, a ghost of who I was.
I just need to get this
— to get you —
off of me.

ENOUGH

Dear mom and dad,
I'm sorry
I wasn't enough.

I'm sorry
I didn't get well
fast enough

      for you.

KEVIN DOHMANN

I have lead
many things
to ruin.
Maybe it's time,
I take myself on
that path.

I'm lying on the floor,
fallen hair around me,
and a razor in hand.
It's poetic, really,
how similar
the two words are:
eraser and razor.
That's what I'm doing,
I'm erasing the traces of you
on me.
I am starting anew.

ENOUGH

I have this irrational fear of abandonment.
I'm always fast to pack my bag
and slow to unpack it.
Always have my belongings at the ready
in case I have to go.
Everything I own fits inside my suitcase.
Started saving money from a young age.
Wanted to take care of myself in case I'm abandoned.

I had this irrational fear of abandonment,
until I wake up,
hand stroking my soft scalp,
eyelids swollen,
and remember.

    It was never an irrational fear.

KEVIN DOHMANN

I walk to Uni
to take the exam.
Wore a hat and
my favorite hoodie
to hide the tufts of hair
I didn't manage shaving off.

I place two pens, an eraser
and a nasal spray on the desk
next to my assigned number.
So if someone asks
why my eyes are red and swollen
I can point at the spray and say
"allergies."

The hardest part
isn't rewriting on the paper
passages from literature
to answer the questions.
It isn't looking everyone in the eye.
It isn't the ache in my chest.
It isn't sitting still
in a room full of people
and silence

with nothing but the sound
of their words on repeat
like songs on my mind.

No,
it's Saga Herrmann.
My name.
It's staring at my last name.
Signing my last name.
The name I share with them.
The name on our letterbox.
The name we were all called
by friends and colleagues.

                It's no longer my name.

When I get home
I fall onto the couch
broken
and so,
so fucking angry.
At my parents.
At myself.
So I scribble notes
into my journal,
letting off the steam:

Since you didn't get it
when I said I'm not okay,
let me clarify:

I'm on four kinds of medications,
I have scheduled meetings
with my therapist.
One every week.
I have to physically force myself to eat
because I forget to.
I am tired all the time
because my brain doesn't rest.

ENOUGH

*When I ask for time
it's not because I want to be mean,
it's because I get panic attacks
as soon as my phone rings.
And you left me
because I didn't have the energy
to call you.
You said things to me
that I hear every second
of every day
and I'm starting to believe you.
And I have to remind myself
I'm not insane.
I have every sentence
in this notebook
to remind me it's true.
To remind me it happened.
To ground me
in reality.
Your words live inside me
as if I'm a fucking amusement park.*

KEVIN DOHMANN

And I have to remind myself
you left your suicidal kid
fresh out of the mental ward
like I'm a piece of trash
and you didn't care
if I'd live or die.
You gambled with my life.
Did you think about that?
Did you ever think about me?

JULY

I wish
someone
holds me
and tells me
"it's okay,
you've fought
for so long
you don't have to
suffer anymore.
You're so strong.
You deserve more
than this pain.
It's okay
to let go."

ENOUGH

Google "how much to overdose and die?"
And then I take a little less than that
to stay alive
but just so.
To feel numb
and make it grow.
"It's for my cats" I say.
"I have no family" I say.
"I don't wanna die" I say.
"I hate being alive" I say.
And maybe it's all of these things.
Maybe I want to punish myself
for everything I don't have
and say I do it for what I do have.
Maybe I am insane.
Maybe the pain is all I am.
Maybe the world is a better place
if I leave now.
Maybe everything in the world
is to punish me.

Maybe I've angered some god.
Maybe I was never meant to be.
Maybe I'm dancing with death
and she holds me near.

KEVIN DOHMANN

Maybe we are in love.
A tragic romance for the legends.
How a child fell in love with death,
spending a life wanting to be united
but always, something comes in between
and when I slip

I am
        still

                out

                      of

                          reach.

ENOUGH

A few days later
my sister calls
and like an idiot
I pick it up.

"Mom is crying," she says,
"she won't tell me what happened,
please fix this,
she misses you."
"I can't," I say.

Because I love myself
too much
to run back into the fire.
To give them another chance
to leave.

"I'm pregnant," she says.
I hate it.
I hate her.
Because this is when she tells me.
This is how she tells me.
Our parents left me
and she wants me to go back
to unite our family
for her kid.

I get it, I do.
But how can she take mom's side
without hearing mine?
Just like dad.

"Wow," I say,
"that's amazing,
I'm happy for you."
Linn's crying so much
pleading again for me to go back.
To call mom.
To try again.
"I'll think about it," I say
and she ends the call.

I hate myself because I
actually hoped she'd ask how I feel.
But she didn't,
I guess she never will.
I hoped she'd tell me
I'm always welcome at her house
no matter what.
But she didn't.

ENOUGH

I can't do this anymore.//
I don't even know what I'm fighting for.//
No one calls me.//
No one checks in on me.//
No one makes sure I'm okay//
like I make sure they're okay.//
And I can hear them rolling their eyes because I call yet again.//
And I can feel them drifting away.//
I can hear them thinking they wish they could stop//
because I'm too much//
      because I'm too broken//
           because my scars are too deep//
and they can't stomach looking at me.//
The pain behind my eyes are all they see.//
They stay cause they know I don't have a family.//
They are my family.//
For me they're the most important people in my life//
but for them I am a drive by.//
I hate this.

I can't do this.

It's too much.

It hurts too much.

Because now I'm not just hurting myself

I'm hurting you too

and that hurts worse.

I need to let go.

        I need to let you go.

                I have to go.

Before I've turned you into someone like me.

Someone who is broken .

This has to end.

                              Or I will.

ENOUGH

People tell me
"don't be hasty,
people always say
what they don't mean."
And I agree,
but another chance
isn't up for grabs,
they didn't leave me
once that week but twice.
I gave them a few days
and their feelings
hadn't changed
so why should mine?

No it's not revenge
it's self preservation
I have a faulty foundation
that I need to build upon.
You can tell me to try again
because you've never walked in my shoes
so how could you

know what it's like to be left without
everything you were taught you deserve.

KEVIN DOHMANN

How would you know?
"Mom" tattooed on your sleeve
and I want to know how that could exist
in the same reality as I am in.
What I wouldn't give
to be you for a day.
To not feel this way.
To know the definition of "parental love"
from more than a lexicon
but deep in my bones
the air in my lungs
but the word doesn't belong to me.

People tell me
"don't be hasty,
people always say
what they don't mean"
when I gave them days
they'd never give me.

ENOUGH

> Mom,
> I grew up
> doing what's best for you.
> I tried my hardest to be the perfect child
> to make it easy for you.
> I hugged and
> I listened to you.
> I partook in your hobbies
> to be closer to you.
> So when I chose myself
> you didn't know what to do.

I won't say a word to our family.
You lost me, I won't let you lose them too.
Guess I'm still programmed
to look out for you.

If someone shows you
their true colors:
don't repaint them.

Dear mom and dad,
I don't trust words,
I don't care for actions
but I believe
in patterns.
You've told me
you're leaving
since I was
a kid
so I shouldn't
be surprised
you did.

ENOUGH

If someone asked me a few years ago
what my greatest fear was,
I'd say "abandonment," "loud noises," and such.

If you ask me today, I'd say:

I'm afraid to exist in peace, to relax and breathe.

I'm afraid to be comfortable
because if I'm comfortable
someone can leave again.
If I try to get better,
I could lose someone else.

I'm afraid that my parents
will understand that their actions
made their sick kid sicker.

I'm afraid to be well.
To be completely well.
To one day live without
my mental pain.
Without my anxiety,
my closest friend,

and my depression,
my oldest friend.
A day where pain
doesn't feel
like my home.

I'm afraid to live
and I'm afraid to die.

I'm afraid
to be remembered
as a number
in statistics.

I'm afraid to meet someone.

I'm afraid to love.

I'm afraid
I'm too sick
to be loved.

I'm afraid
to be seen as sick.

ENOUGH

I'm afraid
to be a burden.

I'm afraid to be angry
because I don't know
who I am when I'm angry.

I'm afraid
of strangers
because it's so easy
to lie to strangers
about who I am
and how I feel.

I'm afraid
of my family
because I'm afraid
they can look at me
and see my pain.

I'm afraid
everyone's lying.

KEVIN DOHMANN

I'm afraid
I'm not important.

I'm afraid
to be important
because if I'm important
they'd feel bad
because I feel bad
and I don't want
anyone to feel bad.

I'm afraid of myself
because I love my pain.
Stockholm syndrome
for my heart and my brain.

I'm afraid
I'm a bad person.
An evil person.
That the darkness inside
want out.
That I'll harm others
unintentionally.
Like I did mom.

ENOUGH

I'm afraid
to be called crazy
because I don't know
what's healthy
anymore.

I'm afraid
my friends don't
reach out
that they
forget me.

I'm afraid
my friends
reach out
because they
deserve better
than me.

I'm afraid
to take my meds
and I'm afraid
to not take my meds.

I'm afraid to sleep.
To have nightmares.
To hear their voices
in my head
as soon as
my thoughts still.

I'm afraid to wake up
and live the same day
again.

ENOUGH

I shouldn't be surprised
my parents left.
I've heard that threat
all my life.

                               Dad came running
                                   into my room.
                                    It was night.
                  I remember it was dark outside.
                        It was dark everywhere.
              "Mom is in the hallway," dad said.
                            He yelled at me
                    because I did something
                      that made mom upset.
                I don't remember what I did,
                  only that one of these times
I thought "she's the one who upset me."
                      "Mom is in the hallway,
                she's leaving," dad continued.
                          "Apologize
                      or she will leave."

                Mom stood in the hallway,
                        bags packed,
                        ready to leave

because of me.
I walked to her,
apologized
and offered a hug.
I assumed it'd be better now,
like the six-year-old I was,
but the threat came
again
and again
and again.

When I moved to a new city,
mom and dad came up
to help me move my stuff.
I told them the day before
that I'd be stressed
this Wednesday afternoon.
"I have an exam
on Thursday," I warned.
Mom presented boxes of things
she bought without asking me.
I got annoyed and said
"I told you not to buy anything
without asking me first."

ENOUGH

When mom went to the car
to drive to their hotel,
dad grabbed my arm
and said,
"don't treat your mom like that,
you upset her."
"I told her not to buy anything,"
I said to which dad replied
"she did it for you."
How did she do it for me
if she did the opposite
of what I asked?

At nine PM,
I was ready for bed
but dad called
and I knew in my heart
I had to answer.
"We're going home now,"
he said. "We don't like
how you treated us
so we're going home.
It's not worth it to come all the way here

only for you to treat us this way."

I had to beg them to stay.
Reminding them I was stressed today.
"I'll prove to you tomorrow
after my exam, that I'm grateful."
It took some convincing
but they accepted my apology,
and for the rest of their visit
I smiled as broad as I could,
saying all the right things
because if I didn't —

if I didn't, I knew they'd leave.

I don't understand why I was so surprised.
It was always just a matter of time.
I guess a part of me believed it was empty words,
just threats.
But now?

Now I know there was always truth behind the words.
When I was six
and mom threatened to leave,
would she have

ENOUGH

if I didn't apologize?
Is there a chance I could've been abandoned
by my mom as a child?
That if I didn't mold myself to fit her needs
she'd get rid of me?

I didn't think my parents
were capable of leaving
their own flesh and blood.

> I was your baby girl
> and you threw me away
> because I decided
> to take care of myself.

This is a new reality.
An alternate reality.
Now I expect all the versions of me
to suffer the same fate.
Now I know what my parents
are capable of,
that there was always truth
behind the cruel words.
I know that if I forgive them,
invite them back into my life,

they'd leave again.
Because the threat
always returned
no matter what I did.
So if they could leave
when I chose my health,
what's to say
next time will be any different.
So I can never go back.

I like to imagine
my life is a book.
Everything I face
is for character
development.
My life is written
in chapters
for dramatic effect.

That's what this is,
I remind myself.
I close the book
of my past,
of the girl I used to be.
I close the book

ENOUGH

of my future.
The future I used to believe in.

I am quick to learn
no one in my family
supports me.

All calls
are to unite me and my parents again.
It's been a month.
A month since I stepped out
of the mental hospital
because I was better
and no one
      no one
            no one asks how I'm doing.

I still hear their words
as soon as my thoughts still.
I still hear
how they said goodbye to me.

I stop eating
again.

I lost the only thing
society
has engraved in me
means forever:
Family.
The only thing
that was supposed to be
unconditional.
Spoiler alert:
it's not.

It's all lies
woven by Hollywood
and Disney.
Happy endings don't exist.
So I'm saying "fuck you"
to the cliches
and tropes out there:
this is my book and
I'm in charge of my story
and I'll make sure it ends happy.

ENOUGH

Am I not enough?
Is that what this is about?
Is it evidence
what you utter to everyone else?
Am I too broken to you?
Are you afraid
I'll tell them the truth?
Is that why you're doing this?

When did I stop
being your kid?
When did you stop
loving me?

When did I stop
being enough?

My sister was turning 20
so I wanted to visit the city.
Called my parents to plan it.
"We can only pick you up
after four PM," mom said.
"I can take the bus,
I still have a key."
That was the wrong thing to say
cause they went quiet.
"We changed locks,"
dad explained.
I moved away two months ago
and the first thing they do
is change the locks on the door.
Of course they did.
"Leave a spare key
under the mat," I force out
pretending to smile.
Another beat of silence.
"Just take a train
that arrives after four."
"Why can't you leave
a key by the door?"
And the truth came out:

ENOUGH

"We don't have keys anymore."
"What?" I asked.
"We have a code lock."
I sigh. "So give me the code
and I'll let myself in."

I didn't get the code.
I never got the code.
Whenever I visited
my childhood home,
I had to be escorted
in and outside
or I'd be locked out.
If the front door
was opened or closed,
dad got a notification.
And no one
thought it was wrong.

Mom and dad took snus
offered by our uncle.
Linn hated it.
It's her birthday, turning 20
exiting her teens
while our parents act
like the teenagers
we weren't allowed to be.
And they're drunk,
taking the tobacco
they swore they'd never touch again.
"It's the hardest addiction
we've ever conquered," they've said.

After midnight
when the party
that used to have "dinner" before it
was no longer Linn's,
she took the bottles
out of our parents' hands
and held up a bin under their chins.
"Spit it out," she said.
Turning 20
a milestone,
the beginning of adulthood,

ENOUGH

ended with Linn
cleaning up the messes
the adults left behind.
I offered to stay
because I didn't want
to drive back to our parents' house
when they're like this.

Linn took mom's car
with us in it
while her boyfriend
tailed us.
Parked outside our childhood home,
with rain pouring down,
Linn left the car and walked
to her boyfriend's,
jumped in and they drove off.
Not checking if we got in okay.
Not checking anything.
She just left, and I understood it.
I understood her.
Her birthday was ruined
like mine always are.

KEVIN DOHMANN

I lock the car,
waiting outside in the rain
while mom and dad went in,
hoping they'd be long asleep
once I went inside.
I was wrong.
Mom yelled at me
the second I closed the door
behind me.
"Sit down," she hissed
from the living room.
I knew she was drunk.
I didn't know what she would do
so I sat down by the table,
dad sat on the couch,
mom stood a meter in front of me and spat,
"Who do you think you are?
You treated us like teenagers
in front of my brother.
We can make our own decisions.
How dare you?"
I didn't tell her it wasn't me
who said or did anything.
I had let them be.

ENOUGH

It was Linn but she wasn't here.
Mom cried and screamed.
I disrespected her.
They were so kind to drive me
to my sister's house
and I treated them this way.

I sat with my face in my hands
sobbing because I was too tired to keep it in.
"Why the fuck are you crying?" she hissed
pulling my wrists away.
So I stood and announced, "I'm going to bed."
Mom kept screaming and dad kept silent.
Just like it always was.
Just like it always used to be.
My bag was still mostly packed,
it would be so easy for me to leave
but I knew tomorrow they'd need me,
their 18-year-old to take care of their hungover selves.
I couldn't leave.
I could never leave as long as they needed me.

KEVIN DOHMANN

No matter
how they twist and turn it
the truth
remains the same.
They told me
their goodbyes
and were upset
I didn't stay.

ENOUGH

I talk to my sister.
She brings up our parents
that I don't talk to them
or of them.
I say "it's unfortunate we don't speak."
She asks "what do you mean?"
She doesn't know the story
of how our parents left me.
She thinks it's the other way around
and I let her believe it.
Because she has what I never will:
parents who stay.
And I'd rather she keeps it.

Forever was ruined in early June.
Parents are only parents
when they need something from you.
It's been one month since you yelled,
called me selfish, and left.
Called off contact with me.
I guess this was always how it had to be.

Was it easy to leave me behind?
To spew lies to our family
to get them all on your side?
Did I matter that much?

ENOUGH

I'm sorry for the twenty years.
I'm sorry I was such a disgrace.
I'm sorry I wasn't enough.
I'm sorry I wasn't harder to leave.
I wish I was hard to leave.

AUGUST

In 2014
when I first came out
mom told me
she'd take me to Pride.
We'd walk together
in the parade
but when the day came —

When the day came
she changed her mind.
She went to the stables
with my sister,
I should've known
she'd throw me away.
After all,
I was never the priority.

KEVIN DOHMANN

Everything broke apart,
that summer day.
You ruined it all
and I got the blame.
It's been two months now,
And it's sad for you,
of course.
Parents who disown their kid
and I should understand
how it feels for you to lose a child
when I lost a family.

ENOUGH

"I don't want you up there alone,"
granny says, "take the train,
I'll meet you at the station."
I don't say "I don't want to"
she won't hear it.
"I'd feel a lot better," she says,
"if you're here with me.
I'm worried about you.
and it would be good for your cats,"
she continues, "to run free for a while."
"Okay," I say and buy a one-way ticket.

KEVIN DOHMANN

For the first time in my life
I'm not at home
in this summer house.
It is no longer a safe haven.

I'm surrounded
by the child me
running around
playing,
living carelessly.

There are pieces
of my parents
everywhere I look.
And granny doesn't want to talk
unless it's about them.

She talks to them
on speaker
in the house
so I can't escape their voices
not even for a while.
I'm trapped,
only safe with my cats.

ENOUGH

I hate white cars.
Because they drive a white car
and they bought it
after the break
so I don't know the registration plate.
I can't check the numbers and letters
to see if it's a match.
So I stand petrified
on the side of the road
staring at every white car
that passes by
because it could be them.
They could force themselves into my life
because they want to.
Because they have
countless times.
Because they'd say they'd leave
if I don't comply
and now that I didn't —
I don't know what they're capable of.

You gave up on me
and put down your foot.
Told me you couldn't be happy
and there was nothing I could do.
You hung up the phone,
told me it's over,
then say it's my fault
we'll never get closure.
I'm just your kid.

ENOUGH

I wake up afraid
and turn off my phone
and hide it under the mattress.
It's my birthday,
turning 22.
And I know
      I know
            I know granny will talk
to dad on speaker
at some point in the day.
Maybe she already does
and I'll go to the main cottage
to make breakfast
and find her deep in conversation
with my father
so he can wish me
a happy birthday.

KEVIN DOHMANN

Granny's sitting on the porch
a cup in hand
so I take my chance.
I climb up the stairs
and greet her.
She grins and wishes me a happy birthday
and dad calls out to me.

It's my birthday
and I feel like a bad person
because dad calls
and I don't answer.
Because I move on
from what they did
and I'm better off
without them.
So I feel like a bad person
for not giving them
another chance.
When I've given them a thousand.

ENOUGH

On my 18th birthday.
I woke up with a smile
and anxiety in my chest.
Maybe I knew what would happen
later in the day.
After school
I took the bus to the city,
met my family
at Hardrock Cafe.
They played Europe
because of course they did.
Mom's favorite Joey
shares my birthday.

We sat in the booth,
mom, dad, Linn and me
for three hours.
The music was loud
giving me a headache.
If they had only asked --
this wasn't for me.
I knew it's not.
It's for mom.

I didn't like this.
All I wanted was a quiet night.
I'd never choose this.
Linn and I sat
in the back of the car
staring out with music in our ears
pretending not to hear
our parents cutting words.
They fight
long into the night.

Mom woke me up
after midnight
sitting on my bed
to apologize.
She gave a monologue
of how she feels bad
for ruining my birthday.
I knew that's not what she wanted
from me.
She wanted me to be her therapist,
to talk her through her emotions,
lending an ear and a shoulder
for her to lie on.

ENOUGH

                              But I'm the kid,
             and this was my 18th birthday.

                              It was never about me.

"Why did you do that?" Granny asks
fire in her eyes.
There's nothing I can say
that will be enough for her.
"You're acting like a child!"
"They left me," I snap.
"The one time I needed them,
they left me."
I wipe the tears from my cheeks,
as Granny rolls her eyes.
"You have to get over it," she says.
"How? Why?"
"Because we're family."
"We used to be a family
before decided to leave me!"
"They've apologized."

"I was only out a few days
from suicide prevention
and I asked for time
and they didn't have it," I say.
"They knew I was hospitalized."
"They didn't know
what it meant," Granny retorts.
"You should've explained it
to them."
"No," I say,
"They're the parents,
they knew I was hospitalized
at a mental ward.
If they didn't understand
what it meant,
they should've looked it up."
"They wanted to hear it
from you," granny says.
"And when I don't give them
what they want,
they leave," I say,
"yes, I've learned my lesson now."
"You can't be serious," she says.

ENOUGH

I buy a last-minute ticket
and pack my bags.
"You can't be serious," Granny says.
"You were the only one
in my entire life
who was on my side.
Who supported me."
I take a deep breath,
looking away.
"My parents left their suicidal kid
and you used to be a therapist
but still you take their side,
knowing I tried to take my life
not that long ago.
Today was supposed to be
a happy day for me
but again you chose them over me."

KEVIN DOHMANN

Sometimes
I'm convinced
I'm a star
a second away
from going nova
destroying everything
in my path
because how
can I accept
your apology
if I think
you'll be better
off without me?

ENOUGH

I live through that night
every day.
Their words echo in my mind
every day.
I'm on the verge of taking my life
every day.

I don't know if I can take
any more of this.
Fighting
to live a life
I don't want to live.
A lonely life
but it's the only life available to me.
I'm struggling
every day
because of what they did to me.
And really what does it say about me?
If I end my story in the middle,
sick of writing the next chapter,
scared of turning the page.
What does that say about me?
If I leave the world today
the way they left me?

Will I show them they were right?
So I stay alive
because they're wrong.
I do deserve it.
I am worthy.

At least that's what I'm telling myself.

ENOUGH

Last night, I had a dream
a nurse had come to me.
My mom was sick and sad
suddenly I was all she had.
And mom begged me to stay.
When it was me, she walked away.

SEPTEMBER

There's a vastness in my chest.
I hold universes in my palm
wishing I could escape there.

But everyone keeps me grounded
with reminders I can never escape.

KEVIN DOHMANN

Everything for my sister,
that's what I did.
I'd be there
whenever she'd need me.
She knew if she asked
I wouldn't say no.
So I rode my bike
five hours to our grandparents
so she could have friends at home.
And I stayed up past bedtime
'cause she wanted to go
somewhere and photograph.
And I stopped studying
for a final exam
'cause she wanted me
to wingman for her.

But a few months after I moved away
my place at the table
no longer belonged to me.
My sister got a boyfriend
and I'm no longer needed
and no matter what he says to me
I pretend it's okay
because my sister needed me to.

ENOUGH

Now after our parents left me,
I talk to her
about our last name
and she tells me
"It doesn't matter.
You're no longer family."
When I needed her.

KEVIN DOHMANN

Dear Granny,
you can think what you will
but don't accuse me
of ruining our family.
Don't say
I have myself to blame.
Don't say
"try harder."
I have always tried
for them.
To be better
for them.
Have they ever tried
for me?
No.
And you know it too.

ENOUGH

I don't know what it feels like
to be truly loved.

When I was hospitalized
for psychiatric care
there was a girl
about my age who had a boy
by her side
every day.
She was so deep in her
depression that she
rarely left her bed
but still the boy came
and sat next to her
to hold her hand
and he whispered her name.
For days he sat and only
whispered her name.
I can't imagine
having someone
by my side
through anything.

I can't imagine when
it's time for visitors

and having someone
show up to see me
and only me
every day.
Can't imagine
having anyone
that would wake up
and think of me
or text me the first
thing they do.
Can't imagine
anyone could love me.
If my parents
couldn't do it,
then who ever will?

ENOUGH

Are you looking out at the rain
remembering the child you left behind?
Do I ever cross your mind?

Have you cried when someone
says my name?
Am I still the one you blame?

Have you taken down my pictures
from the wall?
Was it a close call?

Do you ever ask yourself now
who I'll be?
Was I easy to leave?

Are you thinking back to the day
you said goodbye?
Does it make you cry?

These are the questions
I will never say

because I'm the one you threw away.

KEVIN DOHMANN

> I used to think I couldn't live
> without you in my life,
> then one day the impossible happened
> and I did,
> because I had to.

It isn't "what doesn't kill you
makes you stronger"
it's "what doesn't break you
makes you wiser."
I am not stronger today,
but I am wiser.

ENOUGH

What hurts the most
is that my family all want
me to go back
to people who played
with my life.

What did they think
would happen?
Mom's first words
after suicide prevention
telling me she's mistreated.
Then telling me
it wouldn't be vacation
if I'm where she is.
Telling me
she can't sleep
because of me.
Telling me
she doesn't know
if she can be happy again
because of me.

Both my parents
ending the call

unsure if we'll
see or hear
from each other again
before hanging up.
They knew
my history
of suicide attempts,
suicidal thoughts,
self-harm,
my depression
and anxiety,
my medication,
that I'm seeing a therapist.
They knew I was hospitalized
for all of it.
But still they said those things
and I believed them.
I believed I was a bad kid
making mom feel mistreated,
that I'd ruin mom's vacation
if I was there with her.
That I caused my mom
so much harm
she couldn't even sleep

without taking pills.
That I sucked the happiness
out of her life.
That I forced my parents
to leave me.

That night
I knew I made a mistake.
I shouldn't have sought help.
If I had gone and killed myself,
mom wouldn't have been mistreated,
she could still sleep at night
and be happy,
have a vacation without me.
It was my fault.
Asking for patience
was asking for too much
and I should've realized it sooner
but I've realized now
I wasn't asking for too much.
If they slowed down
and thought about me
they'd remember
where I'd been

and why I was there
if I mattered to them
even a little bit
my life would've mattered to them.
They'd ask me how I'm feeling.
They'd listen to my side of it.
But at the end of the day
I didn't mean enough for them.
If I meet them again,
there's only one thing
I'd like to know:
after you said those things
to your suicidal kid,
what do you think I did?
What do you think
rationally
that a suicidal person
with the history I have
and that you know about,
will do when their parents
says what you said to me.
What do you think I did?

ENOUGH

And there you have it.
There you all have it.
The reason I can never go back:
they gambled with my life.

OCTOBER

I remember when I first told my sister
I was dating a girl.
She asked which letter
in the acronym I was.
I said "the L".
She stared into the distance
looking everywhere but at me
and then she spoke the words
that forever
distanced us.
She said:
"You're a different person now."
She said:
"I don't know who you are."

What I wouldn't give
to change her reaction here.
To rewrite that moment

and make it happier.
To have her say
"Tell me about this girl
you're dating."
Or "thanks for sharing that
I understand it wasn't easy."

My parents,
my granny,
my sister
are all the same.
So it must be something
wrong with me
since I don't fit in.
Since they leave.
Since they left.

ENOUGH

Germany used to be
something that united my sister and me.
We'd talk about going back
if Sweden goes south.
Rooting for Germany
in soccer,
no matter their opposition.
I remember the game
when Sweden turned
4-0 to 4-4.
Me and my sister
were Germans
the first half,
and when Sweden scored
we'd quiet down.
Disappointed.
When Sweden reached 4-2,
we looked at each other.
After 4-3,
we were converted,
rooting for Sweden.

It's bittersweet,
going into a game,

knowing your team
will both lose and win.

It's bittersweet
because my sister
doesn't identify
as German anymore,
and I have no one
to share this with.
No one who gets it.

My sister and I
are two sides of
the German coin:
one proud of our immigrant past,
the other denying it.
No longer reveling in it.
Was she called a Nazi
just like me?
All I know,
is she doesn't like talking about Germany,
or the Grandpa we never knew.
Not anymore.

ENOUGH

My sister texts me
"I don't know
how to talk to you
anymore.
How to keep in touch."
It's okay, I think,
you never did,
so why start now?

DECEMBER

There's Handball tonight.
Sweden is playing
so of course I'm watching
and of course I'm thinking
of you, dad.
How I used to call you
between periods,
after games,
and how we discussed
the gameplay.

I remember the night
I decided not to call
because maybe,
maybe,
maybe my dad would call.

You didn't.
Of course you didn't.
I should've known.

KEVIN DOHMANN

It hurts looking back on June
knowing dad was okay
leaving me
without listening to me.
That my side
wasn't worth enough
for him
to hear me out.
Mom's perspective
was the only one that mattered.

I'd give anything
to have a mom
whose first words to me
after suicide prevention
had been "how are you?"

ENOUGH

I'd give anything
for a dad
who'd call me
and ask for my side
of the story
before leaving.
I'd give anything
for a sister
because I don't think
I have one anymore.

I'd give anything
so the girl I used to be
was spared.
To build a time machine
and save myself.

KEVIN DOHMANN

I thank the world
for Germany.
For giving me
traditions to partake in,
when the loss of my parents
stained my Sweden.

Meatballs and mini sausages
for Christmas,
replaced by Koulroudale
and Bratapfeln.

But Germany
will never claim me,
I know.
But can't I still
claim it as my own?

ENOUGH

Grandpa was German,
fleeing a war.
I studied German
for six years
before I left home.
I was German
since childhood.
Growing up in a town
where all were proud
to come from places
other than Sweden.

I sewed the black, red and gold
for my first sewing class.
The assignment was
to sew a flag,
either sew our own
or design our own.
I made my second flag,
my grandpa's flag,
the flag of the generations
bearing my family name,
and my classmates made theirs.

KEVIN DOHMANN

> I was German before I would walk,
> you'd hear I was German
> as soon as I'd talk:
> the German "r"
> from grandpa,
> I still have it.
> Proof of my heritage.
> Proof that I am German,
> no matter what people think.

I'm proud Grandpa left a broken country,
instead of believing in der Führer
who broke it.

I'm proud to be German,
because Germany has claimed
most of our losses.
Has claimed the consequences
of a dark time, never denying it.
Floors in museums dedicated to
the Holocaust to prevent it.
I'm proud to be German
even though

ENOUGH

the Germans I see
on the TV
are most likely villains.
Our accent,
our language,
forever stained
by Hitler's legacy
of villainy.
That's why I'm terrified
and quick to speak up
when someone uses
the same rhetoric
as the man who caused
damage to a world,
not just a country.

I can't tell you
how many swastikas
has been drawn
next to my name
in school.
Scribbles calling me a nazi.
I had a friend
who sent me a drawing

of Hitler doing
his greeting.
We're not friends anymore.
Respect the victims
of the war.
We can't reclaim
the swastika,
it's too late to do,
so respect those
around you
who still suffer
from the losses.
We all do.

Germany is proof
the sun will rise
with a new day
and a new chance
to repair itself.

Der Führer wasn't
the beginning or the end,
just a step on the way,
always reminding us
what we fight against.

ENOUGH

When I say
I am German,
that my grandpa,
his mom and brother
fled Germany,
most ask me
the same thing:
were they Jewish,
or Nazis.
And I say neither.
They were German,
a working class family.
So I tell their story,
because refugees
aren't binary.

I am German because
every summer, my parents
took my sister and me
to Germany.
When I have kids,
I'll do the same.
That's the only thing

I take from my parents
to use in parenting.

My home, my hem,
my Zuhause,
is equal parts
tyskt and Schwedische.
So thank you world, for giving me
not just one, but two nationalities.

ENOUGH

I'm sending Christmas gifts to myself.
I've done it since I was a child,
it's nothing new.
It's tradition.
For me it is normal
but I see in your eyes that I'm weird.
That it shouldn't be like this.
That I shouldn't buy things,
wrap them and tie them
to give myself.
You look uncomfortable,
why is that?
You ask if I'm going home for Christmas.
I say "yes."
I say "I am home."
You ask about my plans,
I talk about a night with my cats.
You laugh and say "what about your family?"
I say "they are my family."
So you look away,
no more words to say.
I know it's weird for you
that this is normal for me.
That I don't have any place to be.

KEVIN DOHMANN

No Christmas cards this year.

I hate your silence.
I hate your stiff smiles.
I hate how you're awkward talking about your family
because I don't have a family.
When I'm happy you're happy with your family.
I wish I was.
I wish I could be.
But I found it somewhere else
and I'm happy.
Don't pity me.
Don't apologize.
Be happy.
Be with your family.
I know what it's like to lose them,
so take every moment
before it's too late.

ENOUGH

I cry on the couch
watching *The Grinch*
because for the first time I realize
I have the same backstory as him,
and he got a happy ending,
so maybe I can get one too.

Mom used to tell this joke
but I never found it funny.
She'd say "you don't know
who your father is"
while laughing.
The last time it happened
my sister hissed
"It's not funny!"
and mom stopped

but to this day I wonder
is that the reason
dad didn't fight for me?
It would be so easy
to take a DNA test
and see if Germany
shows up.

ENOUGH

It's not like it matters.
Not really.
He's my dad,
he raised me
and he still left me.
The only thing a DNA test would do
is make me lose Germany, too.

I have happy memories
with my family.
Not just the bad
that I wrote here.
We've traveled together
seeing the world
and I loved it.
We've seen Handball live.
We've had ski trips
and road trips.

KEVIN DOHMANN

I have happy memories.
I do but it doesn't change it.
It doesn't change anything.
Because to them
my good days
weren't good enough.
They left 'cause I didn't get well
fast enough.
I can think about the happy
instead of focusing on the sad
but it doesn't change the fact
they were the ones who left.
The happy wasn't enough for them.

ENOUGH

I get a card in the mail.
It's white
with a pink heart
in the middle.
Inside it says
"Welcome to
the baby shower!"
Signed at the bottom
are my sister
and her boyfriend's names
and the time and place.

I text my sister
"I got the card.
Thanks for the invitation."
"You're coming, right?" she texts back.
I stare at the card
and our parents' address.
My phone dings with a new message.
"It would mean a lot to us
if you could come."
I wonder who "us" are.
The future parents
or are our parents included?
"Of course I'll come," I reply.

APRIL

Look into the mirror
I'll tell you what I see:
someone who is strong
with a kind heart.
You've done your best
with what you got.
You are doing well.
You've done so well.
You're breathing
and that is a victory.
Your heart beats.
Your heart keeps beating life into you.
Your lungs keep breathing life into you.
And that's how you win the war.

Don't stop on broken glass,
when you've come so far.

KEVIN DOHMANN

Hi, mom.
I wish I could say it's nice to see you
but you're crying rivers,
hugging me so tightly
and I'm smiling
saying "it's okay"
but it isn't.

ENOUGH

This is your second chance.
This reunion.
This lunch.
This conversation.
Your arms
around me
suffocating me,
crushing me
into what you want.
I don't belong here.
Sometimes goodbye
is a second chance
and it's time I get mine.

KEVIN DOHMANN

We eat lunch
at our parent's house.
In the house I grew up in.
I hate it.
I spend most of the evening
hiding in the bathroom.
I can't do this.
Surrounded by memories.
By my parents
who pretend like leaving their child
isn't that bad.
"I guess it wasn't that bad"
that's what mom says
and I'm sitting
having dinner
with both of them, my grandparents
and my sister and her boyfriend
and I have to smile and nod
even though they ruined me.
Because if I don't
I'll ruin our family.

ENOUGH

Why do they do this?
Where's my apology?
They're lying
saying this is okay.
It wasn't that long
since they said they didn't want me.
Make up your mind.

KEVIN DOHMANN

>   Mom and I
>   always had sewing projects.
>   Making dresses
>   and shirts
>   together.
>   Except, we were never together.

>   I could talk to mom
>   about sewing the next day
>   and she'd agree.
>   But the next day
>   mom has left
>   before I wake
>   a single note for me
>   with instructions.

>   I never cared for sewing.
>   Not really.
>   For me it was a way
>   to connect to my mother
>   but she never even bothered
>   doing it with me.

ENOUGH

And now she tells me
"we could sew something
together again,
like we used to."

No, mom, I think,
we never did,
'cause you were never there.
Instead, I say "I don't sew anymore."

KEVIN DOHMANN

Everyone comes
to that point in their life.
No matter who you are
or what happens to you.
You breathe in,
you breathe out
and you say,
"That's enough.
I've had enough."

Everyone comes
to that point in their life
when they learn the meaning of
"the straw that broke
the camel's back."

ENOUGH

You want me back
but I'm mean saying "no".
So I'm the one you blame,
after everything
you put me through.
What is wrong with you?
You left.
You walked away
the one time
I asked something of you
and my boundary upset you.

You want me back.
Want us to be a family again,
saying I'm awful
choosing myself.
Did you think of our family
— or me —
when you left?

You want me back.
You.
You.
You.

KEVIN DOHMANN

That's all you care about.
You want me to forgive you
for you.
You left me for you.
But here's the thing:
I'm not you.
I don't want you.
I don't need you.
So thank you
for reminding me
the only ones you care about
are yourselves.
I'm done playing your little therapist,
get help.

ENOUGH

I get it.
You want me to be here.
That's all you want.
As long as I don't speak.
As long as I don't argue.
As long as I sit and nod.
I might not be here.
The way you talk.
The way you act.
Am I here?
I was so used to this
that only the absence
taught me
it shouldn't be like this.

I stood in your shadow
so of course I couldn't shine.

KEVIN DOHMANN

Who am I to you?
Didn't want me at 21
so why want me now?
Mom you're so deep in your feelings
you can't see me
even if I'm right in front of you,
arms wide open,
asking you to see me
but you can't.

Who am I to you?
Have you ever asked yourself
why you've never seen me angry,
never heard me raise my voice?
Why I'm so rational?
Well take a look at yourself:
I'm the stability.
I was the calm in your storm, mom,
but I'm not anymore
because you didn't want me
when *I* was rainy,
when *I* was cloudy
because I couldn't shine a light on you.
Brighten up your day.

ENOUGH

Listen to your problems
and make them feel miles away.

Who am I to you?
Nothing.
Ash and dust
collecting
on the floor
under your feet
as you trampled all over me.
Showing me everything I did for you
don't matter shit.

Who am I to you?
Irrelevant:
who am I to *me?*
I'm a good person,
a kind person
with a lot of patience.
I'm a calm person
because I know the storm will pass
but if it won't
and I will crack
I'm calm because I know

KEVIN DOHMANN

I am strong
and I can take it
even though I wish I didn't have to.

Who am I to you?
Nothing.

Who am I to me?
Everything.

ENOUGH

When the lunch
turns to drinks
it's time.
We move to the living room.
The floor is covered by presents
in pink wrapping paper.
Except for mine,
it is yellow.

"Thank you all for coming,"
my sister says.
"We really appreciate it
and all of you
who took the time
to celebrate with us."
She raises her alcohol-free champagne
and says "To Linnéa ████ Lundin!"

KEVIN DOHMANN

I stare at the floor
my heart racing
and I'm gasping for air
pretending I'm okay
as everyone cheers
and congratulates
the new parents
while one thought
stays in my mind
riding a carousel.

Linn named her daughter
after our mother.

ENOUGH

I don't understand my sister.
How our parents
left me
and she stays with them.
As if she's not worried
they'll leave her too.
Maybe she knows
they wouldn't.
That she isn't disposable.
That she isn't me
"How are you not worried?"
I want to scream.
"The things they yelled at me,
You could be next in line."
But after all this time,
they've threatened to leave me
— but never her — behind.
So of course she's not worried.
She's not like me.

I go up to my sister
and hug her
and say "I'm really happy for you
but I cannot stay."
"Why not?"
"I really have to get home,
just wanted to wish you the best."
Linn smiles and nods
and she says "okay."

ENOUGH

While putting on my jacket
my parents ambush me,
standing on either side of me
in the narrow hall.
"I can't believe you," mom says.
"You're leaving?"
"I have to get home," I say.
"Let us at least give you a ride
and maybe we can talk a little," dad says.
"No," I say and tears slide down
mom's cheeks as she looks at me.
"How can you do this to Linn?
How can you do this to us?"

I was never going to be enough for you.
I am sick of trying
of fighting for you.
You never fought for me.
You had your chance
and you took it to leave.
And dad,
I'm sorry I expected
you to call.
That mom had talked to you,
that she told you
she left me
and you'd call
and ask how I'm doing.
I'm sorry I expected
you to care.

You didn't back then,
so why should you now?

How can I trust
you ever will?

ENOUGH

I sigh. "It doesn't matter,
it's all in the past."

"We can move on," mom says,
"it's like you said, it's in the past."
She tries to hug me but I take a step back.
Away from her.
She cries harder now.
"You can be really cruel you know," mom hisses.
"And selfish."
I nod, smile, and say "I guess I got it from you."

You made me think
I wasn't good enough.
Made me question
my worth
without you
in my life.
But I deserve more than you gave me
and I know that now.

You had me in chains
forcing me down
but now I will soar
like a butterfly
across the yellow fields.
I'm better
since you left me.

I admit I'm not perfect
and that,
dear mom and dad,
is what separates you
and me.

ENOUGH

I'm selfish.
It's okay, you can say it.
I'm selfish
and I'm proud of it.
I'm not used to putting myself first
and I deserve to.
So that's what I'm doing.
I'm selfish.
Doing what's best for me.
I was so used to doing
what's best for you,
it must be so hard for you
to see me put
someone else first.
I'm selfish
for every day I couldn't be.

KEVIN DOHMANN

You haven't been my parents
since the day you told me
I have ruined your lives.
You haven't been my parents
since the day you told me
I'm the reason you won't ever be happy.
Dear mom and dad, you're right
you've lost a child.

ENOUGH

You can't break pieces that are already broken,
but guess what, mom: you're the one who broke them.
You say I should give you another chance
so you can throw it away.
No matter what you say,
you haven't changed
and now I don't expect you to.
You'd never change for me
like you forced me to change for you.
I'm sorry that I'm not sorry anymore.

KEVIN DOHMANN

You walked away
told me I was crazy
thinking you could stay.
Told me I was mean
treating you that way.

You hung up the phone,
told me I'm worthless
as you left me alone.
Told me it's better
if we both let go.

You've come back
told me you're sorry
treating me like that.
Told me "it's good now
let's mend the crack."
You're too late.
Told me things
I will never forget.

ENOUGH

Taught me to stand
and fight for myself.

You walked away
so I stay away.

I picked up every piece
you shattered.
I weathered every storm.
I hugged you as you cried
and listened to your problems.
I was there for you
with kindness and patience
but you left when I needed you.
Saying I had mistreated you.
I was a mess, still suicidal,
still anxious and depressed.
I was just discharged from suicide prevention
and your feelings were of much greater importance
than your child's.

I was your child.
Not anymore.
I weathered that storm.
You threw me away
so now I just have one thing to say:

ENOUGH

I am amazing.

I am kind.

I am funny.

I am patient.

I am an ocean, full of love and light.

I can find beauty anywhere.

I am strong.

I am a survivor.

I am creative.

I am fantastic.

I have botanical gardens growing in my chest

and it must suck for you

because you threw me away.

And I will have to live with that pain

for the rest of my life.

And it must suck for you

to lose your child

when it sucks for me

that it was your choice.

KEVIN DOHMANN

I finally understand,
sometimes distance is needed
in order to see clearer.
You were never there
and you never will be.

> When I was available
> we went weeks without speaking
> if you never called.
> When I placed a boundary
> you crossed it immediately,
> only wanted me when I wasn't available.

You know what's funny?
I can't recall a single moment
when I was alone with you
before I moved away.
You didn't want me
when I was right there
only when I left.
It is always on your terms.
It was always on your terms.
You weren't there for me
so I have to be there for me.
Just because you couldn't choose me
doesn't mean I won't.

ENOUGH

I envy people
who live with their parents
at 20 years old.
I never had that choice
not if I wanted to live.

I envy people
who never worried
about money
or becoming homeless
because they have a support system.
I don't.
I don't know what that's like.
If I fail, I fall.
That's it.
I don't have the privilege
to look at Uni and say
"maybe this isn't for me"
because if I leave
that's it.

I envy people
who are loved.
Who are cherished.
I want to know what that's like.

I envy people
who have help
if they just reach out.
I want to know what that's like.

I envy people
with loving parents
because they won't know
what this feels like.

The more fiction I consume
the more I believe
people like this
actually exists.

ENOUGH

What kind of parent
disowns their suicidal kid?
I tried to take care of myself
so you threw me aside.
I still long to die.
And you will never know
that beneath my broken parts
you shattered a hopeful heart.
I was a robot, before the eclipse
my battery was the child in me
who longed for a life
I will never have now.
So now I'm metal and rust.
Empty and numb.

You disowned your suicidal kid
and really what did you expect?
That I'd crawl back to you
and beg you to stay?
It was always going to be this way.
You've made your threats all my life.

You were the one to say goodbye.
Are you surprised I tried to die?

I couldn't live in this world anymore.
How can one live when their parents
rather leave than nurture you?
A world where my sister told me
I'm no longer family.

These words live inside me.
They are my motivation.
I am living out of spite
so I'll one day live out of love.
I am going to show you
you lost me
as if I was trash
but I know myself to be treasure.
So go ahead, mom, and cry
tell me you regret what you did.
It doesn't matter now.
You did what you did.
This time, you have to fucking live with it.

ENOUGH

I will never be like you.
I will never let myself
fold in on myself
the way that you do.
I will be there.
I will lend my ears
my arms, my heart
to the ones I love.
I'm not you.
I grew up hearing
how much I resemble you.
Well no longer,
I'm stronger than you.
The resemblance ends
skin deep.
You taught me
a parent can leave
so I'll prove to myself
for the rest of my life
that a parent can stay
      and so will I.

KEVIN DOHMANN

If I have
a thousand
chances
to give,
I'm giving
them all
to myself.

I'm planting
my roots
so I can
stand taller,
so I can
reach higher.
I am a force.
You can
step on me
again.
I will
keep
growing.

ENOUGH

You have no idea how many times
I've walked out the door,
imagining I'll never walk through it again.
But I always came back
because you needed me.
You wanted me to be like you.
Mom,
I don't want to walk in your footsteps,
'cause I've seen the damage you leave behind.

This time,
when I close the door behind me,
I know: it's the last time.

       Finally.

This isn't about my parents.
This is about me.

This is about me
realizing my worth.

This is about me
understanding my hurt.

This is about me
choosing myself.

This is about me
forgiving myself.

This isn't about
family.
This is about
making a family
in myself.
This isn't about
home.
This is about
finding a home
in myself.

ENOUGH

I'm not your kid
anymore.
I am my own
child.
I am my own
parent.
I am my own
hero.
I am my own
caretaker.
I am my own
lover.
I am my own
survivor.

This was never about you.

KEVIN DOHMANN

If you ask
how long it's been
since my parents left,
I'll lift a lock of hair
and stretch it out
and say "this long."
You'd laugh and say
"That's not what I asked."
I shake my head.
"I shaved it off," I say,
"after they left
I shaved my head
and haven't cut it
since."

My hair is as long
as I've
been alone.

My hair is as long
as I've
survived.

ENOUGH

The chill air
caresses my face.
Snowflakes kissing my cheeks.
There's no suitcase in my hand
'cause I don't want anything
to be a portal between my two lives.
There's nothing of yours
I want to keep.
The snow creaks under my feet.
Sweden has different words for snow,
this one is kramsnö
'cause when you hug it, press it together,
it becomes solid. A perfect snowball.
I'm hugging the snow
with every step, keeping it together.
The snow and I are one.
Every time you stepped on me,
you didn't break me:

I might creak and cry,
but I solidify.

Shards of glass
turned into a vase.

KEVIN DOHMANN

Bits of coal
turned into a diamond.

I don't turn around,
there's no need.
Because I don't need to see you,
you're behind me.
So I keep walking,
facing north,
moving on.

Yes, I'm walking alone,
but I'm not alone,
I have the stars above me.
Big Dipper forever
watching over me.
I'm not alone,
I have me,
and this time it's enough.

I am enough.

I always was
and I always will be.

AUTHOR'S NOTE

My life changed forever
early June 2019,
just like Saga in the story
my parents left me too.
Her journey of self-discovery
and healing
is very much based
on what went on inside me.
Though our stories intertwine
my recovery took a longer time.
The time it takes
to recover from trauma
isn't linear,
it isn't dependable,
it isn't known.
Each of us deal with it
on our own pace.

And that's okay.
There's no limit
to how long you can grieve.
Or how long you can be burdened
by horrible horrible dreams.
It takes the time it needs.
If you're like Saga and me
I have but one thing to say:
you are enough.
You were always enough.
It's not your fault
if others are too blind to see.
I know it's tough,
I know life seems insurmountable,
and it's hard to remember it's not.
But most of all I want you to know:
you are not — and never will be — alone.

30 SONGS

1. "Piece by Piece" by Kelly Clarkson
2. "You're Exhausting" by Beth Crowley
3. "I Am Not Nothing" by Beth Crowley
4. "Good Enough" by Jana Kramer
5. "You Don't Get To" by Kenny Chesney
6. "If I'm Being Honest" by Anna Clandening
7. "A Light To Call Home" by Julia Brennan
8. "Second Chance" by Shinedown
9. "I Will Survive" by Gloria Gaynor
10. "DNA" by Lia Marie Johnson
11. "Hey" by Andreas Bourani
12. "Would Anyone Care" by Citizen Soldier
13. "You Broke Me First" by Tate McRea
14. "You Ruin Me" by The Veronicas
15. "Born Without A Heart" by Faouzia

ABOUT ME

16. "I'll Be Good" by Jaymes Young
17. "Empty Words" by Beth Crowley
18. "It's Just Me" by Blue October
19. "Lies of My Fears" by MaRynn Taylor
20. "Never Be the Same" by Jessica Mauboy
21. "Deine Nähe tut mir weh" by Revolverheld
22.. "Done" by Beth Crowley
23. "Ist da jemand?" by Adel Tawil
24. "Until It Happens to You" by Sasha Sloan
25. "Should Be Loved" by Blue October
26. "Heal Me" by Grace Carter
27. "Made For These" by Jimmie Allen and Tim McGraw
28. "Control" by Zoe Wees
29. "Love On Myself" by Felix Jaehn and Calum Scott
30. "I'm Doing Fine" by Mike Waters

Kevin Dohmann is a trans guy, living in a small apartment in Northern Sweden. In his spare time he enjoys watching YouTube videos, reading, watching TV and cuddling with his two cats. He'd drop anything to watch Handball, Biathlon or Hockey if Sweden or Germany competes.

Kevin also has his own YouTube channel where he talks about books and about his experiences with being a child of toxic parents.

Where to find Kevin:
YouTube: Much Ado About Books
Twitter: @Kevin_MAAB

CPSIA information can be obtained
at www.ICGtesting.com
Printed in the USA
BVHW042313020822
643675BV00002B/38

9 789198 771039